Behind the Scenes Tour of the Kirtland Temple: From Basement to Bell Tower

By Ronald E. Romig

I0088163

John Whitmer Books

Independence, Missouri

2019

For Kirtland Temple Builders
and Caregivers

Behind the Scenes Tour of the Kirtland Temple: From Basement to Bell Tower
By Ronald E. Romig
Copy edited by Lavina Fielding Anderson, Rene Romig and Marilyn Lamoreaux.
Special thanks to: John C. Hamer, Lachlan Mackay, and Barbara Walden.

"History of the Kirtland Temple Behind the Scenes Tour" by Barbara Walden, former Kirtland Temple Visitor Center Director, 2002-2009; currently serving as Director of Community of Christ Historic Sites Foundation.

John Whitmer Books, Independence, Missouri
jwha.info

ISBN 978-1-934901-20-5

Library of Congress Control Number: 2017918832

Printed in the United States of America

Cover design by John C. Hamer.

Table of Contents

HISTORY of the BEHIND-the-SCENES TOUR

By Barbara Walden, Community of Christ Historic Sites Foundation Director

FROM THE MOMENT THE early Latter Day Saints raised the walls of the Kirtland Temple, people have been fascinated with Kirtland's "House of the Lord." Members and non-members alike travel thousands of miles for an opportunity to explore the magnificent historic site that towers over the surrounding landscape.

"Behind-the-scenes" tours are not a new experience, as they have been happening at the Kirtland Temple from the 1830s. Wilford Woodruff recorded his amazement following a tour with Warren Parrish in November of 1836. He recorded in his journal that the splendor of the lower court and view from the bell tower were highlights of his temple experience, feelings that resonate for guests today 180 years later.

Twentieth century "Behind-the-scenes" tours of the Kirtland Temple began in the spring of 2006. Although tours of architectural exploration were happening frequently among the historic site staff throughout interpretive training sessions, the tours in the spring of 2006 were our first formal invitation to the Kirtland community to join us on a tour experience previously not offered to the public. Our first guests included LDS missionaries from Historic Kirtland and members of the Kirtland Kiwanis Club.

A formal interpretive outline was created and soon the tour experience was entitled "From Basement to Bell Tower." The two to three hour tour highlighted the architectural significance and beauty of the historic house of worship. Descending into the basement to view the original beams and stone walls, entering into the crawl spaces and climbing to the bell tower gave guests a unique perspective and understanding of the labor and ingenuity of the early Saints.

The tours also gave the Kirtland Temple staff an additional opportunity to spot any maintenance or preservation concerns. It is fairly common for bell towers in northeast Ohio to fall into disrepair, for example, not because the church isn't being cared for but because caretakers don't frequent the bell tower nearly as much as other parts of the building. Our "Basement to Bell Tower" tours gave us an opportunity to not only educate guests on the architectural history of the Kirtland Temple, but also to help us better preserve and care for the National Historic Landmark.

It is in this collaborate spirit of education and preservation that I hope the "Basement to Bell Tower" behind-the-scenes tour continues long into the future.

Kirtland Temple Bell Tower, 1903.

Overview of Artifacts

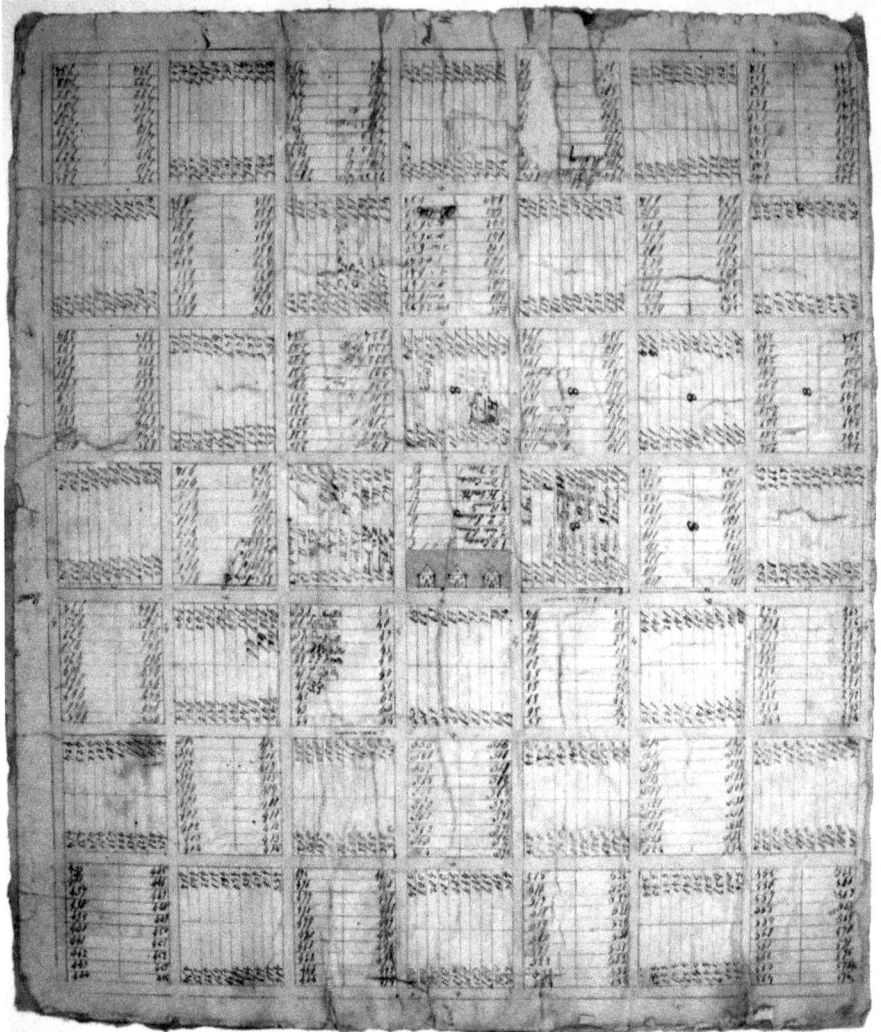

Plat of the City of Kirtland, 1833.

This drawing reveals plans to build three buildings the size of Kirtland Temple at the center of the community. The first floor of all three of the buildings would have offered assembly halls to provide spaces where the community could worship and hold meetings.

THE KIRTLAND Temple is but one of three large public facilities with which Joseph Smith Jr. proposed to grace Kirtland's Public Square during the Mormon period.

The second level of the building in the center of the city plat was to provide space for church administrative activities.

The second level of the southernmost facility was to house the church's printing operations. Instead, Joseph set up his office in the attic of the temple. Also, a temporary printing office was built right behind the Temple, almost up against the back wall. Much of the early literature of the church was first printed in that little printing facility.

Center detail of the Plat of the City of Kirtland.

Mural overview of Kirtland, ca. 1890.

Quorums of the Twelve and Seventy were also first organized in that building.

Kirtland Temple was both the spiritual center of the Latter Day Saint community and the city's meteorological center. Kirtland was an intensive agricultural community. Its weathervane helped residents determine when to plant and harvest their crops.

Kirtland Temple weathervane details.

THE BACK HALF OF the original Kirtland Temple weathervane nearly rusted through and was removed from the top of the finial in 1993. While forging the weathervane, a Latter Day Saint blacksmith probably started with an iron bar, then hammered it out into a flat sheet. Uneven hand cut marks may still be seen along the edges where a cold chisel was used to cut the finished shape.

The top coat of the stucco that covered the walls contained

Rubble stone wall covered with stucco.

pieces of broken glass and crockery. As a result, the temple sparkled on sunny days. This early stucco was on the building for many years.

Walls and Stucco: The walls of the building were built out of small stones known as rubble stone and covered with a coat of stucco.

IN THE 1830S, TEMPLE builders traced thin dark lines upon the surface of the stucco to complete the illusion from a distance that the building appeared to be constructed of large smooth polished blocks of stone.

The original stucco had begun separating from the building by 1955 to such a degree that it had to be replaced with a modern white Portland cement stucco to protect the building. It has been white as it appears today since about 1960.

Kirland Temple stucco showing surface lining.

Above: Circle plaster sweep. This tool was used to construct the smoke rings above the chandeliers in the lower court. This tool was used again in the 1970s when the surface of the vaulted ceiling was restored.

Smoke ring: The circles on the ceiling of the lower court contained hooks at the center from which to hang chandeliers. Smoke from burning candles would rise to the ceiling where the smoke rings trapped the soot and kept it from depositing on the whole ceiling. As a result, it was not necessary to clean the ceiling as often.

Sprinkler head: A modern sprinkler system has been added to help protect the temple from possible fire threats.

Below: Compaction grouting core sample. This core sample was produced during the process of stabilizing the temple foundation. This process is known as compaction grouting.

ORIGINAL TEMPLE exterior window frames and glass hang on either side of the entrance to the Theater in the Kirtland Temple Visitor Center Gallery. Caretakers removed the windows in the 1980s to protect the frames from further deterioration due to exposure to the weather. Rather than lose the original window frames to the ravages of the elements, staff removed the original frames and stored them. Replacement windows duplicate the original frames, and reproduction glass evokes the correct historical appearance.

In the 1830s, manufacturers could not pour glass as is done today. Glass was formed beginning with a blown bottle shape that was flattened and spun out in a disk as far and as thin as possible. Makers then snipped the hot glass into individual panes of glass. Each pane contains two layers of glass—two walls of the bottle surface collapsed together. That is why light passing through is so diffused. Visitors may see where traces of the spinning process adorn the surface of many of these early panes of glass.

Original Kirtland Temple window.

Finial: This structure sat atop the Kirtland Temple for many years above the bell tower. The weathervane was fastened on a long metal rod that ran up through the center of the finial. The finial was removed in 1993. A replacement made of spun copper now sits atop the bell tower. The front portion of the original 1830s weathervane was in good enough condition that it was remounted and may yet be seen turning above the finial.

Pulpit windlass: This roller is part of the temple curtain or veil system. It was installed under one of the pulpit benches and allowed pulpit occupants to raise or lower pulpit enclosures.

Temple Exterior

Exterior foundation wall and quoins.

LARGE STACKED stones or quoins (ornamental blocks) on the corners of the temple help hold the weight of the massive stone walls in place.

The front door steps have been replaced at least twice, each time with similar sandstone and dressed in the same decorative style as the original steps. An early engraving by Henry Howe, drawn in 1846, shows the temple steps one step higher than today.

The area in front of the temple was an extension of the road. Carriage drivers could drive right up to the temple's steps to drop off passengers.

Corner protectors were installed before the 1887 RLDS Conference to help prevent wagons from running into the building's corners.

The placard sign board above the east-facing doors notes the change of the name of the church in 1834 from Church of Christ to Church of the Latter Day Saints.

Photographs of the temple's exterior features are permitted, but please refrain once we are inside the House of the Lord.

East exterior wall tablet showing original content.

Many early Saints lodged in the Kirtland Hotel, located directly across the street from the temple, operated by Sidney Rigdon's son-in-law George Robinson. Photo by George Edward Anderson, 1907.

Outer Court of the House of the Lord

Outer court of the House of the Lord.

UNLIKE OTHER NINETEENTH-CENTURY meeting-
houses in northern Ohio, the pattern for the Kirtland Temple was stimulated both by revelation and scripture. Joseph
Smith and other church leaders experienced shared revelatory experiences indicating the size and appearance of the building. As the building
progressed, these leaders described their understanding of the edifice to
its builders. Their awareness of the temple in Jerusalem also guided the
arrangement and function of the House of the Lord's interior.

Inner Court: House of Worship

THE BEHIND-THE-Scenes tour of the temple begins in the basement and ends in the bell tower. While ascending, the tour explores many of the structure's non-public spaces. The temple basement is little more than a four-to-five-foot-deep hand-dug space situated below the temple's sanctuary. In the basement, tour participants can look up through the floor joists of the lower court and examine the underside of the Melchisedec pulpits.

Before the tour descends the temple basement stairway, it is helpful to review the more familiar appearance and organization of the Melchisedec pulpits as viewed from the lower court level. These details provide context for an examination of the arrangement of the underside of the pulpits. The temple pulpits are original.

In 1873, Joseph Smith III, son of Joseph and Emma Smith, born here in Kirtland in 1832, acquired title to the temple. And, Smith's RLDS followers began worshiping in the temple.

Melchisedec pulpits of the lower court of the House of the Lord.

Frederic G. Matther sketch of modified Melchisedec Pulpits, Kirtland Temple, ca. 1875.

As originally constructed, there was a narrow aisle at the front of the sanctuary between the pulpits and pew boxes. Joseph III did not live in Ohio and spent little time in Kirtland. To provide a bit more flexibility, RLDS worshipers modified the first level of the raised Melchisedec pulpits and removed the front panel and table of the pulpit. This afforded worshipers a better view of the floor and seating area of the elders' pulpit. Following their removal, the pulpit's front panel and table were stored temporarily in the basement.

Throughout the 1870s, an early church member named Rebecca Dayton lived near the temple in a little red house located across Maple (Whitney) Street. Her house lot is now part of the cemetery. Rebecca, who often served as the temple tour guide, was not happy with this change to the pulpits and wrote to RLDS President Joseph III requesting permission to restore the pulpit. She got the approval and hired a carpenter to reinstall the front of the elders' pulpit.

Sometime later, the sacrament or communion table was re-shaped to resemble an oxen yoke. The RLDS congregation, meeting

Sacrament or communion table in the shape of an oxen yoke.

Joseph Smith III, ca. 1876.

Metal shaft for curtain or veil handcrank.

up the pulpit side stairs, one at a time on each side. You may look into each of the four levels of the pulpits, affording a better understanding of pulpit construction and function.

We invite you to open the door of the second pulpit from the top and view the seating area. Note the metal shaft protruding from the center of the base of the bench. This shaft was designed to accept a hand crank used to raise or lower the pulpit curtains or veils. This is the crank that Joseph Smith Jr. used to lower the curtains during the appearance of Christ in the Melchisedec pulpits.

Also, you may examine the

in the building for regular Sunday worship, also removed the front pews to make room for singing groups and Sunday School exercises.

Visitors usually are not allowed access into the pulpits out of respect for those who occupied them during the 1830s. But, we invite BTS tour participants to remove their shoes and climb

Veil rope system ran under the pulpits, through the columns, and out through the ceiling.

operation of pulpit door hinges. Because the outside surface of the pulpit doors are not flat, but are decorated with several layers of molding, the top rail of the door was cut in a curve to allow the hinge to turn freely. The doors are articulated, like the doors of modern cars, to keep the mouldings from binding.

By 1883, the floor of the lower court of the temple had sagged eleven inches. The floor had to be raised up back to its original level to restore the proper operation of pulpit doors. Today, we maintain the floor at its initial level to ensure the proper function of pulpit doors.

The pulpits are also part of the lower court's curtain or veil system. Tour guides may remove the cover of the heating system's air return register at the base of the south side of the stand, revealing where ropes passed under the base of the pulpits and into the ceiling support columns on either side. These ropes continued on up over the vaulted ceiling and re-emerged through small holes located in the ceiling where they attached to the lower-court curtains.

Large white fluted columns, spaced along sanctuary aisles, are another prominent feature of the lower court. These columns sit atop stone piers in the basement. In addition to concealing the ropes of the curtain system, solid interior beams in the columns help support the weight of the temple's massive wood roof.

Yet another notable feature of this hall is the lovely vaulted ceiling over the center of the room. This feature significantly improves the acoustics of this space and aids the transmission of light through east and west windows. A graceful valance decorates the north and south edges of the vaulted ceiling. Though this design element now covers modern electrical lighting fixtures, it

Lower court vaulted ceiling and valances.

originally provided air circulation into crawl spaces above the lower side sections of the ceiling.

Before exiting the lower court, also note the four large plaster rings and hooks on the ceiling. They held chandeliers which illuminated evening services. These plaster rings helped keep the ceiling clean by trapping soot from burning candles. The plaster sweep tool on display in the Visitor Center Museum was used to create these flowing plaster rings.

Look at the railings running along the side stands. We believe that there were railings at the time of the temple dedication, which at some unrecorded point were removed. Before the 1887 RLDS General Conference, held in the Kirtland Temple, building caretakers restored the missing railings. RLDS Presiding Bishop George Blakeslee turned the railings and spindles in his home workshop in Illinois and shipped them to Ohio by railroad in time for the 1887 conference.

Lower court fluted columns.

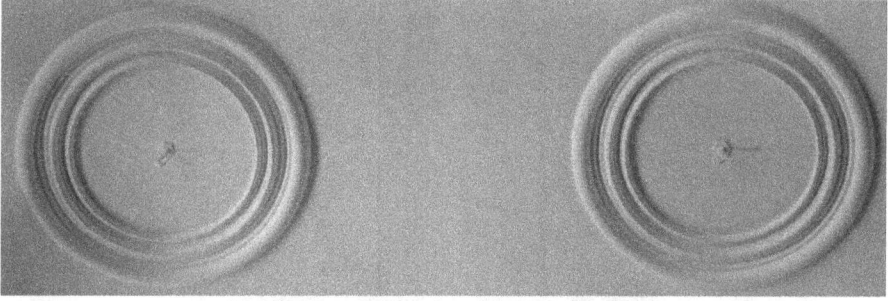

Lower court ceiling chandelier smoke rings.

Kirtland Temple Basement

NEXT WE'LL EXIT the lower court and move to the basement. Here you will put on hardhats to protect your heads and get flashlights that will help illuminate dark corners.

Initially, access to the basement was through an exterior door on the south foundation wall near the rear corner of the temple, but we'll enter the basement from the outer court. In 1836, there was no central heat in the temple, but, in 1837 temple caregivers installed heating stoves in the four corners of the temple basement.

An interior entry doorway to the basement was concealed beneath the Aaronic pulpits at the east end of the lower court. Temple caregivers believe this door was not part of the temple's initial 1836 construction, but think this retrofitted interior basement door was added to provide internal access to the basement when the heating stoves were installed.

Close examination of this door reveals early construction methods identical to other temple doors. The boards in the temple doors are joined together by a mortise (a pocket cut into a beam to accept a tenon) and tenon (a projection on a board or beam cut to fit into a mortise) technique. Wooden pegs held the assembled boards in place. So, the basement door looks very much like temple doors built in 1836.

Support beams under the Aaronic pulpits have been retrofitted, providing an important clue that this opening in the outer court wall did not exist in 1836. With the interior basement door open, participants can see how Aaronic pulpit support beams have been repositioned. The original placement of support beams would not have allowed the basement door to open.

During retrofitting, new mortise notches were cut into the pulpit joists. The original beams were repositioned eight inches farther away from the pulpit side

Temple basement door.

Pulpit support beams have been modified.

of the outer court wall. This modification confirms the absence of this door when the pulpits were initially built.

While constructing the foundation, builders created the opening for the original basement door in the temple's south wall. The basement may not have been completely dug out until after the temple's walls and timber skele-

ton were finished. Evidently, the basement had been excavated by the time builders began constructing the bell tower's stone support piers. Certainly, the basement had been dug out by 1837 when the four heating stoves were installed in the basement's corners. However, throughout the three-year process of building the temple, the exterior basement door provided the only access to the building's cellar area.

During the 1837 installation of the interior basement door, builders also added an interior stairway to the basement. They removed one floor support joist to accommodate this new basement stairway. As you descend these steps, look for a mortise cut into the main support beam above the

Temple exterior basement entrance door at southwest corner of the basement.

Interior basement stairway.

bottom stair step. Originally, a floor joist fit into this notch. The mortise pocket is large enough that a person's fist can be inserted, but please look only!

One of the temple's main floor support beams runs directly above the last stair step. This remarkable walnut beam was cut from a single tree and spans a distance of about sixty feet from one side wall of the temple to the other. The presence of such

Mortise notch in main foor beam.

Temple main floor support beam.

Axe.

Adze.

a beam in the temple means that builders were able to find a tree in the surrounding forest that was more than fifteen inches in diameter at a height of sixty or more feet above the ground. Because the tree was so large, builders were able to square the log off from one end to the other into a finished timber beam fifteen or more inches in width. Though rare today, there were many such old growth trees available in area forests in the 1830s. Indeed, builders found not only one tree of that size, but they located, cut, and installed a total of seven beams like this to support the first floor, seven more for use on the second level, and seven more to crown the walls at the roof line.

Trees cut to construct the temple had to be harvested about one year before use and seasoned, either by soaking in water for about six months or by heating in a lumber kiln to drive out the sap. After seasoning, logs were shaped or sawn into usable forms.

Marks are easily visible along the surface of these huge support beams where an axe or adze was used to shape them by hand. Builders inserted both ends of these hewn beams into the stone walls before they were erected. Builders could not construct the wall above beam level until these vital structural members were in place.

Even though each beam appears massive and strong, builders cut a series of notches into them along their tops on both sides from one end to the other to hold floor joist tenons. Thus, though these beam appear solid, they are really only as strong as the intact interior uncut portion—about six inches wide—through the center of the beam.

It is believed that Jacob Bump, an early temple workman, supervised laying these floor beams. This was no doubt Bump's largest building project ever. The building crew made a major mistake by laying the main floor support beams the wrong way. The widest part of the beam was laid sideways leaving only a narrow part of the beam to support the weight of the building. Six inches of solid beam is really all that is holding up the weight of this heavy building at this point. Today, we know it should have been laid the other way with the thickest part positioned vertically.

In April 1834, Artemus Millett, an experienced builder, arrived from Canada. It is believed Millett guided builders in setting the beams supporting the second floor in the right direction.

Two lines of stone-support piers were constructed in the basement to both support the floor beams as well as help hold up the weight of the heavy wood roof.

Next, the tour moves to the center section of the south foundation wall. Hyrum Smith was in charge of the temple building committee. Jared Carter and Rey-

Basement stone support piers.

nolds Cahoon assisted Hyrum in managing the work of the committee.

In the summer of 1833, Hyrum Smith led a group of men to his wheat field where Hyrum dug the first shovelful of dirt from the foundation trench. Before long, workmen had completed a trench that was several feet wide and about five feet deep. Next, workmen laid cornerstones and began hauling stone from local quarries for foundation walls.

In 1933, the RLDS Church commemorated the laying of the cornerstone of the Kirtland Temple. Community of Christ church history reports that commemoration leaders opened the cornerstone and found and removed a penny. Today, we do not know where either that cornerstone or penny is located. We are not even sure what early church builders meant by the term cornerstone. Did they mean the four stones in the corners of the first layer of the foundation? Nothing like a corner stone is visible at each internal corner of the basement foundation wall. Nor is an ornamental stone visible at an outside corner of the building. However, one dressed stone appears in the middle of the south foundation wall near what would have been the top of the foundation wall. It would be interesting to know whether the center of this stone is hollowed out.

You can see that the bottom of the basement windows sit at ground level. The foundation wall does not run into the ground much deeper than the window—only about four to five feet more. The foundation wall continues only a few inches further where it reaches the level of the dirt basement floor.

The temple is not built upon solid stone bedrock, but rather upon glacial deposits of sand, clay, and gravel. The last great ice age that covered this part of Ohio ended around 12,000 years ago. When the glaciers retreated, they left behind a vast plane of deposits about forty feet deep. The temple was erected atop this rather unstable material. Northern Ohio regularly experiences minor earthquakes. During such events the temple rocks atop a virtual puddle of sediment. This geologic flexibility may have served the temple well over the years, making the temple walls relatively stable. However, we wish temple builders had provided a more extensive foundation.

Originally, before builders dug out the basement, there was dirt on both the outside and inside of the foundation walls—pushing in equally. Structurally speaking, digging out the basement was probably a mistake. Foundation walls no longer had dirt supporting them from the inside and began to "toe in" at the bottom from the greater pressure of the earth pushing in from the outside of the foundation. Consequently, the walls began to

Dressed foundation stone, south wall.

Diagram: Dirt pushing in from one side

Concrete piling added to support the ends of floor beams.

Floor beam, wall pocket, and piling detail.

support the ends of the massive floor beams.

Just above eye level, you can see where one of the large main floor beam girders rests in pockets in the outer stone wall. Also note fluorescent paint spots along some of the beams. These paint marks, dating from the 1990s, are laser survey landmark points. The building is surveyed every five years or so to monitor building movement. Caregivers have found the temple to be quite stable since the foundation has been stabilized through compaction grouting.

Next we'll move from the foundation to the southwest corner of the basement to better examine a main floor support beam coregirder. The RLDS Church held five general church conferences in the Kirtland Temple, the first in 1883 and the last in 1904.

During the 1904 RLDS general conference, a main floor support girder cracked. This beam supported the front section

open wider at the top. You can see the impact of this imbalance as you examine the exposed stone walls in the crawl space between the first and second floor. We will also explain the actions that have been taken at that level to minimize the further widening of temple walls.

To firmly stabilize the temple's walls, in the 1990s Community of Christ building caregivers employed a technique called compaction grouting. They forced concrete under the foundation walls under pressure to create a network of cement that now supports the walls of the temple better than when it was originally constructed. They also installed large concrete pilings along the inside of the foundation wall to

Kirtland Temple survey marker.

Main floor beam crack showing repair under lower court.

Sections of tree trunks support the floor.

Stone wall and exposed floor joists under lower court Melchisedec pulpits.

of pew boxes in the southwest corner of the lower court allowing the floor to sag several inches. The session of conference was suspended as attendees exited in great alarm. Workmen created a secondary beam by hewing a tree log and inserting it directly beneath the crack. They also jacked the floor back into place. Subsequently, a metal brace has been installed at the location of the crack in the original beam and a series of tree log support posts were added under main floor beams to prevent further collapses.

We next move to a position under the Melchisedec pulpits. With the aid of flashlights aimed up through the main floor joists, you can examine the underside of the Melchisedec pulpits. Temple workmen knew that no one would ever walk around under the raised pulpits, so they didn't waste any wood by installing flooring under the pulpits. As a result, you can look right up through the floor joists to view the underside of the pulpits.

You can also see the inside of the temple's exposed exterior stone wall. Builders did not plaster the exterior wall's inner surfaces beneath the pulpits either. About half of the exterior window is covered by the pulpits, so tour participants can also see the bottom sill of the large south-facing exterior window. The bottom of the south side pulpit stairway is visible to your left.

Further left is the underside of the side stand floors. To the right, use your flashlights to illuminate the underside of the north side stand, with steps ascending to the various levels of the side stands at either end. Note the large wooden pegs, used to connect the pulpit's support infrastructure.

Next, focus on the flooring materials. A good example appears just above the level of the floor joists at the extreme north end of the side stands. At first builders installed a thin construction floor. Later, on top of the first layer, they installed a second, thicker set of finished floor boards.

Some unique features of the building and some temple artifacts may be seen from this vantage point. On the floor, hidden behind some boards, are plaster moulds, built in the 1940s by temple custodian Earl Curry, that were used to fashion lighting sconces installed on the outer walls of the lower court to hide modern electric lights. Under the pulpits, near the back wall of the basement, participants can also see two stove heat collectors. These collectors may not be from the earliest heating stoves used in the basement, but confirm that the stove pipes that originally ran up through all three levels of the temple were eigthteen inches in diameter.

Next, you'll move back to the far left, almost to the exterior

Underside of pulpit sidestand stairs.

Wood pegs fasten pulpit support beams.

Sub-flooring and finished flooring boards.

Extra sconces designed by Earl Curry stored in the temple basement.

Stove collectors accepted pipes eighteen inches in diameter.

basement door. Here, stored on the floor are some of the original stone door frame members that were removed in the early 1990s. Original stone door frames were held in place with iron metal pegs. An original stone door frame base

Metal pegs in stone door frame base.

may be seen on the floor. Two iron pegs protrude from the top surface.

Over the years, moisture slowly seeped into the crack between the stone base and frame materials causing the metal pegs to rust. Pressure from the expanding rust made the vertical stone door frames start to split, so caregivers had to replace the stonework around the doors. Inert pins, not susceptible to rust, now hold the new installation in place.

Along the south wall, a retrofitted iron beam has been installed atop a series of floor jacks. These jacks were introduced to keep main floor joists from separating from mortise pockets in the exterior stone wall.

Next, we'll enter a more modern enclosed area of the basement extending to the north basement wall. Earl Curry, temple caretaker from the 1930s through the 1960s, used this workspace to facilitate many needed temple repairs and restorations.

Along the bottom of the outer wall, you can see where concrete was added underneath the north temple foundation. This difficult repair work was done by hand, digging under the foundation and reinforcing the space under the wall.

Also, along the exterior north wall you can see the temple's heating manifold, a central part of the building's modern heating system. To eliminate open flames

Melchisedec pulpit jacks.

Earl Curry's temple basement workshop.

in the building from stoves or furnaces, efficient heating units were installed outside along the north temple wall. The manifold channels heated and cooled air throughout the building via heat exchangers and blower fans.

As we leave Curry's workshop, we move toward the northeast corner of the temple basement. In the 1920s, RLDS stewards minimized the threat of open flames in the temple by piping hot steam from steam boilers in a building across the street. A tunnel under the Chillicothe Road pumped heated steam to the temple. After the installation of the temple's current heating system, the steam heat tunnel was no longer needed. The tunnel itself remained in place until recent utility installation trenches across the street cut it off.

Temple air handlers.

Blocked off basement steam pipe tunnel.

Sprinkler system pumps.

A memorable incident occurred during a behind-the-scenes tour in 2006. Interpreter Barbara Walden was explaining the steam tunnel to a visiting family from Canada. The grandmother of the family was very interested and started moving toward the tunnel opening. Her grandson said, "Grandma, don't go back there." Grandma replied she really wanted to get closer and kept walking. Her grandson pulled her back, then pointed to a live blacksnake hanging down the door of the nearby sprinkler system pump room. At this point, Barbara paused to call the maintenance staff. When she turned around after the call, her tour group had disappeared. They climbed right up the basement steps and continued on outside. The tour was over.

When another family from Canada visited the temple a few months later they asked if they could take the snake tour. Now, with the tunnel closed, snakes can no longer get into the temple as easily.

As you walk to the bottom of the basement steps, notice pieces of wood sticking through the ceiling overhead. They look a bit like clothespins. These boards are connected to the pew boxes

Clothespin-like anchors through floor.

Aaronic pulpit banister fastener.

Pulpit railings.

sitting on the floor above. This same feature will be visible when the tour explores the crawl space between the first and second floor. We'll explore more details at that point.

However, a similar wooden piece protrudes through the floor close to the basement stairway. This round peg is held in place with a wooden wedge. This item is the end of the wooden newel post of the stairway banister railing running along the south side of the Aaronic pulpit stairs. Similar railings run along the

Abandonded center bell tour support pier.

north side of the Aaronic pulpits, as well as either side of the Melchisedec pulpits.

Notice the row of five stone piers arrayed before the temple's east basement wall. While constructing the bell tower, original builders knew that the stone exterior wall of the temple would support the weight of the front portion of the bell tower. But, builders needed a way to support the back portion of the tower, along with the additional weight of a bell. The smaller of the stone piers, in the center of these five piers, was started to help support the west end of the bell tower.

When builders began installing large glass windows to admit light from the front light well into the lower and upper courts, they quickly realized that they could not transfer the weight of the bell tower through glass windows. This fact rendered the center pier unusable. No weight rests upon it. Indeed, you can pass your hand between the top of the pier and floor joists. This center pier was simply abandoned and builders installed two additional stone piers on either side of the space occupied by the windows.

We have now concluded our exploration of the basement. Please wipe your feet thoroughly before entering the outer court. The basement lights are normally turned off and the basement door kept closed during regular tours.

Outer Court Stairway

Keep your hardhats and flashlights in hand as the tour ascends to the crawl space between the first and second floor. Tour participants climb up the outer court stairway single file and enter the south crawl space between the first and second floor.

Crawl space entrance.

Bench for BTS tours in crawl space.

Crawl Spaces

THE BEHIND-THE-Scenes tour guide will demonstrate a method for negotiating the hand railing as tour members enter this non-pub-lic area, either climbing over or crawling under the railing.

Your hard hat will come in handy because a sprinkler pipe is located right above where you begin to raise up. You must also avoid an exposed light bulb that hangs from the ceiling joists. Pro-vided benches give you a place to sit during the tour guide's expla-nation.

The inside of the exterior stone wall is clearly visible here in the crawl space between the first and second floors of the temple. These exposed stone walls are an example of 1830s rubble stone construction. Rubble stone construction involved building

Interior of rubble stone wall.

Pockets in stone wall hold up crawl space floor/ceiling joists.

Long rods and turnbuckles help stabilize stone walls.

an outer wall and an inner wall from moderate sized stones and then filling in the space between the two walls with smaller-sized rubble stones.

The stones were held together with mortar. Typical lime mortar from the 1830s is so soft you can brush it off building materials easily with your fingertips. But apparently Artemus Millett knew the secret of making a much more durable mortar. The temple's mortar has held its stone walls together securely over the years. Modern Portland cement, commonly used in brick or stone mortared walls in our day, became available in the United States in the late 1860s.

Looking closely along the edge of the wall, you will see where builders also set the structure's floor/ceiling joists into pockets in the stone wall. These joists were once firmly seated in and fully filled these pockets. But over the years, movement has gradually caused the joists to pull out of these pockets. Today it is possible to insert your hand into the empty pockets beyond the ends of the joists. These openings may reflect some shrinkage of the wood beams but are related more to the movement of the walls over the years. The distance between the temple's outer walls has gradually gotten wider. If this tendency had been allowed to continue, ceiling joists would have pulled completely out of their respective wall pockets. The lower court ceiling could have collapsed.

In the 1950s, Earl Curry installed long metal rods, equipped with turnbuckles, through the temple's outer walls. These rods

Temple caretaker Earl Curry.

Added floor joist support brackets.

were installed through each end of the building and at each level, tying the north and south walls together, while others connected east and west walls. This procedure slowed the widening at the tops of the walls, but did not stop it completely. It was not until after the completion of compaction grouting under the foundation that the walls were finally stabilized. It appears that the movement of the walls was halted just in time. Some of the joists now sit upon an inch or less of stone and temple caregivers regularly check for further movement.

To further stabilize the

Main beam support brackets.

building, metal hangers have been retrofitted along the length of the wall so that joists will not collapse, even if they should come out of their wall pockets. Restorers also installed metal brackets at the end of each ceiling joist where tenons fit into the mortise cuts of matching main support beams.

While examining the ceiling joists, notice a pattern of vertical saw marks along each side. Many of the boards in the temple were cut by hand. Men worked in teams of two. One man would

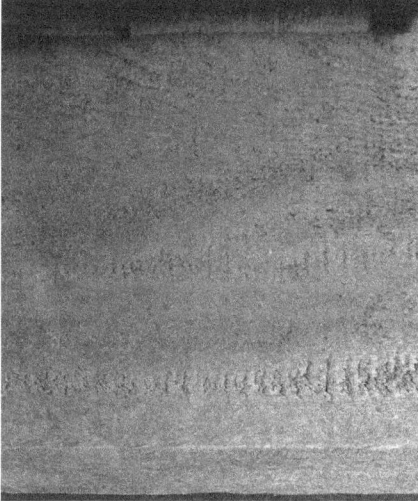

Crawl space floor/ceiling joist showing vertical saw marks.

operate a pit saw while standing above the timber while another worked from below. This was very labor intensive. Subsequently, church members constructed a mechanical reciprocal saw at the bottom of the hill near the Chagrin River. Much mechanically sawn lumber also was incorporated into the temple.

Also notice additional clothespin-like pieces of wood protruding through the ceiling. They are support boards designed to hold the pew boxes in place on the floor above. Pulpits could be lifted up off the floor if needed. Corner pew boxes face north and south, while center pews run east to west.

Participants may also notice pegs sticking out from the framed wall next to the stairway. These pegs were used to tie stairway stringers to vertical wall studs.

Pew box anchor.

Running through the center of the building, from east to west, are curved wooden forms. These curved forms were constructed to support the plaster of the vaulted ceiling of the room below. Small strips of wood called lath were attached to the lower face of the forms. When builders installed plaster on the ceiling below, some of the wet plaster squeezed

Main stairway support beam peg.

Tail ends and lath and plaster detail.

through the open spaces between the laths. After it dried, excess plaster worked like fingers to help hold the covering in place so the heavy plaster would not fall from the ceiling

While building the vaulted ceiling on this level, workmen began neatly trimming off the tails of the curved wooden forms toward the front of the building. However, some crew leader must have reminded them that this was not meant to be a public area, so no one would be examining the work. As unintended visitors to this space today, tour members can look down the row of ceiling

Curved lower court vaulted ceiling form.

forms and can see where form tail ends were left uncut further on down the row.

Beyond the modern furnace plenum that now also occupies this crawl space, you can see the first of several main support beams. On this level of the temple, the support beams are much larger than the support beam in the basement. Artemus Millett was supervising the construction by the time this beam was set in place into the rock wall. Artemus knew that main beams needed to be larger. Millett also made sure

support beams were installed properly, with the main thickness running vertically, to support the massive weight of the building. Additionally, Millett incorporated angle braces into the beam construction to better distribute the weight.

Near the northeast end of the building, a rope guide related to the building's veil system is visible along one of the vertical support beams. Ropes intended to operate the curtain or veil system ran up into this crawl space alongside this beam. This intricate rope

North crawl space between second and third floor support beam.

Support beam.

Lower court Aaronic pulpit rope guides.

guide, fastened onto the beam near the top, merits closer examination: channels carved through the guide direct each passing rope to a different destination over the vaulted ceiling. Near the east wall of the outer court, you can see a block of wood with a hole drilled through it. The wood block served as a guide to redirect its rope through the ceiling above the Bishops' pulpit where it attached to a roller and a related curtain. Three additional blocks served the same purpose over the other pulpits.

We move from the crawl space to the upper court.

Opening through ceiling for ropes.

Rope guide above LC Aaronic pulpits.

Pulley above UC Aaronic pulpits.

Rope guide above upper court Aaronic pulpits.

Original pew boxes in the southwest corner of the upper court.

Upper Court: House of Learning

WE WILL BEGIN this portion of our tour in the southeast corner of the upper court. Joseph Smith referred to this level of the temple as the House of Learning.

The pew boxes in the south corners of the upper court are original. Each are equipped with study desks set in a fixed upright position. We had seen the ends of the pew back support boards protruding through the ceiling of the crawl space below. Each pew box divider wall has two sets of equally spaced boards fastened on its front and back. These boards, which fit through notches cut into the floor, hold the pew boxes in place.

Caregivers also believe that the pulpits on this level of the temple are original. Tour members may see an indication of this by looking at the backboard of the bench in the third level of the Aaronic pulpits. This wide board is a slice of wood cut from a large tree. The marks along its surface were made by a workman's hand plane. This is how boards were made in the 1830s and modern builders can't get boards like that.

Truman Angell supervised the construction of this level of the temple in 1836-1837. The 1830's side stands and center pew boxes were somehow removed at

Hand plane markings are visible on the backs of upper court Aaronic pulpit benches.

Upper court Aaronic pulpit side stand backboards date from the 1880s.

Upper court pew boxes are absent. The Windsor chairs provided seating from 1887 to 1918.

some undocumented point. In the 1880s, the upper court side stands were reconstructed and used during RLDS general conferences. You can see that the boards used to reconstruct the backs of the side stand benches are much narrower and uniform in width than the southeast corner bench back.

One source indicates that, in the 1850s, planks were installed across the backs of the original pew boxes creating a raised false floor. Researchers discovered a lovely 1907 photograph showing the upper court filled with Windsor chairs. Note their distinctive curved backs. In 1918, RLDS temple minister A. E. Stone

reconstructed the center pew boxes. Following church leaders' instruction to make seating able to face either way, Stone installed hinges on study desks in the center sections, allowing desk tops to be lowered out of the way. As you can see, the boards used to construct the backs of the pew boxes are uniform in width and even narrower than those used in the side stands.

As a revealing anecdote, Earl Curry recorded that, during his thirty year tenure as temple maintenance man, he would devote about an hour sitting in the southwest pulpits on this level and praying before starting each

Then we'll leave the upper court. Watch your step. There is an immediate step down.

From the outer court, look at the large Palladian style window that illuminates the inner court. This is identified as "the Window Beautiful." By standing against the outer wall, you can more easily see this window's lovely intricacies. First, look at the regularly shaped rectangle panes in the two lower window sections. Panes of glass used throughout the temple were available only in a single standard size at that time. Next, look at the irregularly shaped panes of glass in the top section of the window. Focus on the small cracks in these glass panes of the fan light at the top. These joints are not the result of vandalism or the building's movement. Rather, because sections of the fanlight are larger than the standard pane size, workmen had to install two and three pieces of glass end to end to fill in these larger openings.

Handcranks on the side of upper court columns operated windlasses and ropes activating the curtain or veil system.

Panes of glass pieced end-to-end fill in large fan lights atop the Window Beautiful.

work day. Earl indicated that, as a result, he avoided a lot of maintenance mistakes.

We will walk past the west pulpits and pause in the north aisle, so you can examine the rope and windlass system inside the columns designed to operate the curtain system.

The Window Beautiful.

Here in the outer court, RLDS workmen cut a door through the wall into the space under the Aaronic pulpits in the 1940s to install a fire hose. In the 1950s, workmen installed sprinkler pipes and sprinkler heads throughout the building. This protective sprinkler system was recently updated with modern sprinkler heads.

Next, the tour guide will lead you in single file up the stairway to the attic floor.

While climbing the stairs, you'll see another crawl space between the second and third floors.

Fire hose storage in upper outer court.

Ceiling sprinkler head.

Sprinkler head and pipe in crawl space.

Joseph Smith established his office on the building's upper floor. He set the church in order from there, and called the attic level of the temple "the House of Order."

Crawl space between the second and third floors.

Attic-level floor boards.

Attic Level: House of Order

THE HOUSE OF Order portion of the tour begins at the back of the building in Joseph Smith's office. The original flooring on this level of the temple is composed of variable board widths. In the northeast corner of the room, you can see where one of the eighteen-inch stove pipes ran up through the floor. Part of the curved pattern of the pipe is still visible in the flooring. Another pipe ran vertically through the other end of this room. These pipes continued through the ceiling into the supra-attic space above. Two pipes joined at this end of the building and two at the front merged into two short brick roof chimneys. Most exterior photographs of the temple show the building with these two chimneys. The temple had no central heating when it was built, so initially there were no chimneys.

Stove pipe patch in the floor of Joseph Smith's office.

Slate from 1880s-1970s temple roof.

Around the turn of the Twentieth century, RLDS Church workmen replaced the old wooden shingle roof with a slate roof. It proved to be a mistake in the long run. Slate lasts longer but is much heavier than wood shakes or shingles. Before long, the roof dormers began to sag. In the 1950s, Earl Curry installed steel beams beneath the dormers to support their lower part. While doing so,

Doors under the dormer windows.

Joseph Smith's office in the west end of the attic floor level.

Curry shortened the width of the room about three feet by moving the north and south walls in eighteen inches each.

Open the door at the north side of Joseph's office to see the steel beam. Then look at the shelf below the dormer window to see where the original sill ended. In our day, workmen filled these crawl spaces with insulation to help with temple heating.

Earl Curry also installed a smaller beam to support the top end of each dormer, then adjusted

One of the steel support beams installed by Curry.

Chimneys were visible in many historic images of the temple, ca. 1898.

the ceiling line to conceal this support structure.

When the RLDS Church decided to replace the slate roof with shakes about forty years ago, the chimneys were removed to restore the building's original profile.

Temple roof dormers admit much light into these attic rooms, while interior windows serve the same function. As you move toward the front of the attic, note the large oval window frame displayed in the middle attic room.

This is the original window frame from the attic's front wall. The glass is not original. This window originally had glass pieced together with many small cracks between the standard size panes.

Look at the sliding window in the front room. Originally it contained smaller panes. During the summer, worshipers could open windows in lower levels, this window, and the bell tower doors. The resultant updraft would have functioned something like a whole-house cooling fan, a great

Original oval window frame.

cooling option for the summer, but Saints of the 1830s had no similar simple solution for heating the building during winter.

Next we come to the bell tower entry area. Notice the trap door in the floor, the first of four trap doors that provide access to

Interior bell tower window.

Attic floor interior windows.

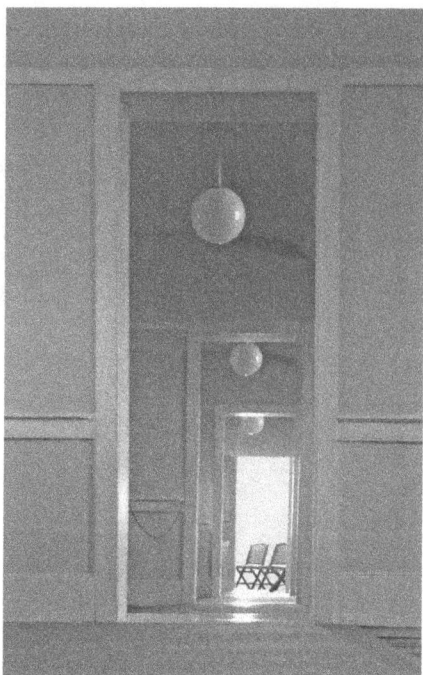

Attic floor hallway showing four rooms.

Joseph Smith's office before the dormers were reinforced.

Bell-tower-level trap door.

the bell tower.

Early Saints were unable to install a bell during the 1830s. Around 1890, RLDS Apostle Gomer Griffith had a dream, leaving the impression that the church should install a bell in the House of the Lord. Gomer and RLDS congregational leaders began to raise funds for the purchase of a bell. A major event was a lawn fete in the yard of the temple. The Willoughby High School Band played, and the gathering garnered three hundred dollars. This sum was not enough for a new bell, but as Griffith was traveling in southern Ohio on a mission, he stopped at a Cincinnati, Ohio, foundry. The owners told him that a new bell would cost much more than three hundred dollars. They showed him a

Second trap door.

bell that another church had ordered, then decided not to install. Griffith bought that bell for three hundred dollars. It was transported to Kirtland, unloaded in the outer court, and pulled into place through all four trap doors using a block and tackle. The thousand pound bell has a lovely tone.

Apsotle Gomer Griffith.

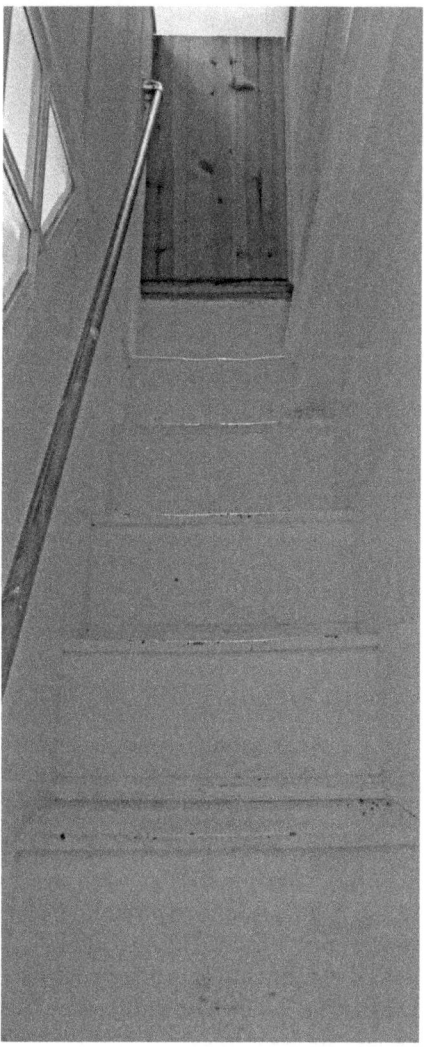

Attic-level bell tower stairway.

Visitor Center staff ring the bell fifty times every Sunday morning at 9:00 a.m.

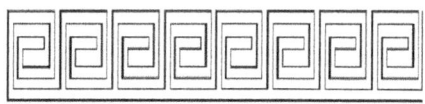

Bell tower west window.

Kirtland Temple shake roof from the bell tower's west window.

Bell Tower Level

EVERY TOUR OF THE temple before 1950 included a trip to the bell tower, but structural engineers asked the building guides to stop taking people to the bell tower because the weight could stress the tower. The tower has since been strengthened.

BTS participants will climb up into the bell tower. The guide will turn on the light switch halfway up the bell tower stairs on the west wall and lead you upstairs to the next level. Here you may look out of the window in the west wall of the bell tower and view the temple's wood shake roof.

At this point, you are about fifty-five feet above the ground. Below is the cemetery. Also note the five dormers lining either side of the roof. The dormers were repainted during the summer of 2010. The roof's end gables and bell tower were also repainted.

Some of the roof shakes were replaced in 2010. Roof shakes last about twenty-five years. The current roof shingles have been in place for about twenty-five years. Temple builders originally installed sawn shingles, so temple caregivers are considering replacing the current roof with sawn rather than split shakes.

You can see lightning rods along the roof line. The first rods were installed in 1847. Since then, the temple has been struck by lightning many times, but these devices have saved the temple from fires by dissipating the electrical charge safely to the ground through copper cables. The current rods are replacements. Remember that there were no chimneys along the roof ridge line, although many historic photos show two brick chimneys.

Open the small door below the window frame and shine your flashlight into this open space. This is the temple supra-attic, directly above Joseph Smith's office level. Notice the large support beams that help hold up the roof. This part of the attic was never intended to be a public area, and workers seldom go into this space. It is filled with insulation to help with temple heating.

Walk carefully and keep your hard hat on as you follow your tour guide up the steps to the next level of the bell tower. The steps get narrower the higher you go. Another sprinkler pipe is located at the top of the stairs just where it seems safe to stand up.

Don't stand on the trap door. If the weather permits, the trap door overhead may be opened to reveal the underside of the bell.

The temple has been on fire more than five times. Around 1882 workmen were covering the bell

Door to the supra-attic.

Final stairway to the bell tower.

Stairway to the tower deck.

Original lath at the top of the stairway.

Trap door directly below the bell.

Kirtland Temple bell.

tower roof with copper sheeting. Bishop E. L. Kelley was away, but his wife, Cassie, was watching the work progress from the porch of the Kirtland Hotel across the street. Cassie noticed that workmen had carelessly started a fire with their metalworking torch; she ran throughout the neighborhood, and organized a bucket brigade. The fire was extinguished before too much damage occurred.

The bell tower was struck by lightning in 1904 and caught on fire. Again, a bucket brigade was successful in extinguishing the

Cassie Kelley.

Bell tower copper roof.

fire, but this time the tower suffered substantial damage.

Fortunately, the RLDS Church had insurance coverage which reimbursed repairs. During the renovation, tower workers worked on the support beams. Though some of the superstructure of the bell tower is twentieth century, the large vertical support beams still show hand hewn markings, signifying 1830s construction.

Portions of these beams also had to be repaired in 1904. Since the bell tower is open to the weather, moisture can seep down its six main support beams then wick up through the wood from the bottom. The bottom of each support beam had deteriorated—rotting from the center out,

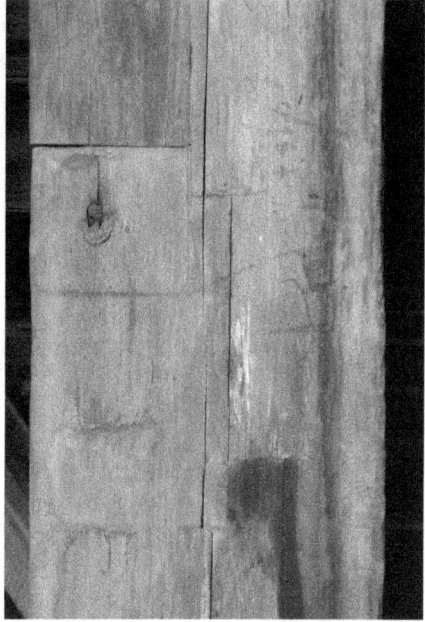

Hand-hewn bell tower support beams.

Splice at the bottom of a tower support.

Splice in a support beam.

Third trap door in the floor of upper tower room.

weakening the tower structure. Had this damage not been repaired with splices at the bottom of each beam, the tower could have collapsed from the weight of the bell. The 1904 restorers cut off the damaged ends and spliced in solid sections at the bottom of each beam. In this way, much of each original support beam was preserved.

Some of these original hand-hewn beams bear initials carved into them either by workmen or by early visitors. Perhaps the M. H. was carved into one of the beams by Martin Harris, who remained in the Kirtland area giving tours of the House of the Lord until 1870. Perhaps the HS just below represents Hyrum Smith, who served as chair of the

Initials carved in the tower support beam.

temple building committee.

You can see where restorers replaced some of the siding along the exterior walls of this space. This made the bell tower a bit wider which helped improve the visual balance between the tower and the building.

Notice the saw marks on the beams supporting the trap door under the bell. Here you can see circular saw cuts, not vertical saw

Replacement tower siding.

Circular saw marks are visible on the trap door support frame under the bell.

Signature of B. F. Miller, Raymore, Mo, April 7, 1904, on a trapdoor support beam.

marks. This is an indication that these boards were not manufactured in the 1830s, suggesting that the bell tower may have undergone a significant amount of reconstruction from this point upward. Markings left by visitors on these boards all date from after 1904.

The tour guide will open the hatch to allow access to the tower deck level, but Community of Christ Risk Management does not allow participants to climb onto the deck itself. The railings around the deck are for decoration only. You must stop at the top step of the ladder. The view is dizzying, but you may steady yourself by holding onto a provided metal pipe hand-railing along the bell enclosure. One person at a time can climb to the top step and look outside. Here you may

View out of the bell tower hatch.

take a photo of the landscape; but even in these non-public spaces, we remind you of our request: No interior photos. From the hatch, you can see the Kirtland Mills burial ground to the northeast and the ridge along the north side of the Chagrin River.

As we begin to descend from the bell tower, note the hole in the exterior wall of the tower's lower room. While painting the bell tower in the 1990s, painters laid tarps on the temple roof. That night, automatic timers turned on the tower spotlights installed on the roof, igniting the tarps. The Kirtland Fire Department re-sponded and quickly extinguished the flames. Firemen chopped that hole in the exterior tower wall to ensure there were no smouldering embers inside.

Temple caregivers regularly repaint the temple, endeavoring to maintain the structure in as much of its 1830 condition as possible.

The temple bell tower, roof dormers, and roof gables were repainted in 2011.

The Behind-the-Scenes Tour ends with the descent from the bell tower. Thank you for your interest in the Kirtland Temple.

Bell tower railing.

Kirtland Mills Burial Ground viewed from the bell tower.

Firemen chopped this hole in the interior tower wall while extinguishing a fire in 1993.

Scaffolding on the temple in 2011.

Thank you for helping preserve the Kirtland Temple.

You may contact Community of Christ Historic Sites Foundation to enquire how you may further assist with the preservation of the Temple:

Community of Christ
Historic Sites Foundation
P.O. Box 338
Nauvoo, IL 62354
217.453.2246

http://www.historicsitesfoundation.org/

Temple Builders

Kirtland, 6 June 1833

This day called a conference of High Priests, 6th June 1833. Bro Joseph opened by prayer. Orson Hyde being nominated a clerk for the presidency of the High Priesthood, seconded and duly chosen by vote, and took his seat to act. The occasion of the conference being called, was this: to council the committee who were appointed to take the oversight of the building of the House of the Lord. These are the names of the committee: Reynolds Cahoon, Jared Carter & Hyrum Smith. It was voted by the conference that the committee proceed immediately to commence building the House or obtaining materials, stone, brick lumber &c.

–Kirtland Council Minute Book, 15.

Kirtland, March 7th, 1835

This day a meeting of the Church of Latter Day Saints was called in this place for the purpose of blessing in the name of the Lord those who have heretofore assisted in building by their labor & other means, the House of the Lord in this place. The forenoon was occupied by Pr. J. Smith Junr. in remarks to the Church upon the propriety and necessity of purifying itself. In the P.M. the names of the [of] several, those who had assisted to build the House, were taken and further remarks were made by President J. Smith Junr. He said that those who had distinguished themselves thus far by consecrating to the upbuilding of said House as well as laboring were to be remembered. That those who build it should own it, and have the control of it. . . .

President Sidney Rigdon was nominated to officiate in laying on hands in the name of the Lord to bestow the blessings.

The Presidency were blessed and Reynolds Cahoon, Hyrum Smith & Jared Carter, the building committee. The last were not present, but their right in the House was preserved.

Names of those who were blessed in consequence of their working on the House of the Lord in Kirtland and those also who consecrated to its upbuilding:

Sidney Rigdon
Joseph Smith Junr.
F. G. Williams
J. Smith, Senior
Oliver Cowdery
N. K. Whitney
R. Cahoon
Hyrum Smith
Jared Carter
Jacob Bump
Artemus Millet
Alpheus Cutler
Asa Lyman
Josiah Butterfield
Noah Packard
Jonas Putnam
Isaac Hill
Edmund Durfee Sen.
Edmund Durfee Junr.
Gideon Ormsby
Albert Miner
Ira Ames
Salmon Gee

Peter Shirts
Isaac Hubbard
Horace Burgess
Dexter Stillman
Amos F. Herrick
Mayhew Hillman
William Carter
William Burgess
Giles Cook
M. C. Davis
Jaman Aldrich
John Young Senior
Ezra Strong
Joel McWithee
Matthew Foy
James Randall
John P. Green
Aaron C. Lyon
Thomas Burdick
Truman Wait
Edmund Bosley
William Bosley
William Perry
Don Carlos Smith
Shadrach Roundy
Joel Johnson
Oliver Higley

Sabbath morning, March 8th, 1835
Pursuant to adjournment, the
Church met for the purpose of further
blessing those who had assisted in building
the House of the Lord. . . .

Evan M. Green
Levi Osgood
Alpheus Harmon
Joseph C. Kingsbury
Ira Bond
A. H. Brewster
Samuel Thompson
John Ormsby
Luman Carter

John Smith
Samuel H. Smith
Thomas Fisher
Starry Fisk
Amos R. Orton
Alman Sherman
Warren Smith
Moses Bailey
Sebe Ives
Andrew H. Aldrich
Ebenezar Jennings
Oliver Granger
Orson Johnson
James Lake
Wm. Redfield
Cyrus Lake
Harvey Smith
Isaac Cleveland
Wm. Barker
Samuel S. Brannan
John Wheeler
Henry Baker
Wm. Fisk
Henry Wilcox
George Gee
Lorenzo Young
David Clough
James Durfee
Joseph Coe
Thomas Gates
Loren Babbitt
Blake Baldwin
Joseph B. Bosworth
Gad Yale
John Johnson
John Tanner
Henry G. Sherwood
Sidney Tanner
Joseph H. Tippits
Robert Dugley
Erastus Babbitt
Samuel Canfield
Phineas H. Young

Samuel Rolfe
Calvin W. Stoddard
Josiah Fuller
Erastus Rudd
Isaac G. Bishop
Roswell Murray
Benjamin Wells
Nehemiah Harmon
Oliver Wetherby
Thomas Hancock
Joshua Grant
William Draper
Ransom Van Leuven
Tunis Rappallee
John Reed
Samuel Wilcox
Benjamin Johnson

Reynolds Cahoon, Jacob Bump and Artemus Millet were then blessed with the blessings of Heaven and a right in the House of the Lord in this place, agreeably to the labor and expense they have performed on the same. Alpheus Cutler, Asa Lyman & Josiah Butterfield were next called, who received the like blessing. The right here spoken of is according to each man's labor or amount of donations. . . .

—Kirtland Council Minute Book, 14-16.

—Fred C. Collier and William S. Harwell, eds., *Kirtland Council Minute Book* (Salt Lake City, UT: Collier's Publishing Co., 1996).

KEYSTONE AT EAST WINDOW

www.ingramcontent.com/pod-product-compliance
Lightning Source LLC
Chambersburg PA
CBHW031540040426
42445CB00010B/624